THE WILD WEST

THE PONY EXPRESS

by Amy C. Rea

Content Consultant
Dr. Robert J. Chandler
Former Senior Research Historian
Wells Fargo Bank

Core Library

An Imprint of Abdo Publishing
abdopublishing.com

abdopublishing.com

Published by Abdo Publishing, a division of ABDO, PO Box 398166, Minneapolis, Minnesota 55439. Copyright © 2017 by Abdo Consulting Group, Inc. International copyrights reserved in all countries. No part of this book may be reproduced in any form without written permission from the publisher. Core Library™ is a trademark and logo of Abdo Publishing.

Printed in the United States of America, North Mankato, Minnesota
042016
092016

Cover Photo: Ed Vebell/Getty Images
Interior Photos: Ed Vebell/Getty Images, 1; GraphicaArtis/Getty Images, 4; Museum of the City of New York/Corbis, 8; Red Line Editorial, 10, 29; Bettmann/Corbis, 12, 30; North Wind Picture Archives, 14, 37; Everett Historical/Shutterstock Images, 17, 45; Aresium Art/Shutterstock Images, 19; Keystone/Getty Images, 22; Bob Balestri/iStockphoto, 25; W. H. Hilton (fl.1862)/ Private Collection/Peter Newark American Pictures/Bridgeman Images, 28; Timothy O'Sullivan/ Library of Congress, 32; Corbis, 35; Nat Farbman/The LIFE Picture Collection/Getty Images, 39

Editor: Marie Pearson
Series Designer: Ryan Gale

Cataloging-in-Publication Data
Names: Rea, Amy C., author.
Title: The Pony Express / by Amy C. Rea.
Description: Minneapolis, MN : Abdo Publishing, [2017] | Series: The wild West
    | Includes bibliographical references and index.
Identifiers: LCCN 2015960507 | ISBN 9781680782592 (lib. bdg.) |
    ISBN 9781680776706 (ebook)
Subjects: LCSH: Pony Express--History--Juvenile literature. | Postal service--
    United States history--Juvenile literature. | Frontier and pioneer life ((U.S.)--
    Juvenile literature.
Classification: DDC 383/.1430978--dc23
LC record available at http://lccn.loc.gov/2015960507

CONTENTS

MAIL FROM EAST TO WEST

Johnny Fry waited in Saint Joseph, Missouri, for a very important train. It was 5:00 p.m. on April 3, 1860. A crowd waited with him, excited to see him greet the train. The train held mail to be taken to the West Coast. Fry would take the mail from the train and start a dangerous, fast-paced horse ride. His ride would launch the first speedy overland mail delivery to the West Coast.

Pony Express riders traveled quickly to deliver the mail.

No one knew if the ride would go well. No one had done it before. Fry was expected to ride as quickly as he and his horse could to Seneca, Kansas, about 80 miles (130 km) away. There they would meet the next rider.

The train was delayed. It did not appear until nearly 7:00 p.m., two hours late. But by 7:15 p.m., Fry was ready to go. A cannon boomed, and the crowds cheered. He took off as fast as his horse could carry him.

The Early Days of Mail

Today in the United States, mail is delivered every day of the week.

PERSPECTIVES
Limited Capacity

With only one horse and no wagon, the Pony Express riders could not carry very much. To make sure they could go as quickly as possible, no horse was allowed to carry more than 165 pounds (74 kg). A rider could not weigh more than 125 pounds (56 kg). Each rider had a mochila, a leather case to carry the mail, that weighed 20 pounds (9 kg) when full. Most riders also carried a water sack, a horn to announce their arrival at the next station, a Bible, and one or two guns.

Services such as UPS and FedEx deliver letters and packages overnight. Technology such as e-mail makes moving information from place to place faster than ever before.

But in the early 1840s, these services and technologies did not exist. There were no telephones or computers and no delivery vans or cars. People living in the eastern part of the United States had some technological benefits. Train tracks and telegraph lines went as far west as the Mississippi River. Getting mail and messages from the East Coast to places such as Missouri was not difficult, though these systems were not as speedy as the ones in use today.

However, anywhere west of the Mississippi was a challenge. Without railroad tracks and telegraph lines, it was very difficult to get messages and letters to the West Coast. In the early 1840s, mail from the East Coast to California did not go across the United States itself. Instead, it was sent on a ship

Clipper ships sailed around Cape Horn to deliver mail to the East and West Coasts.

that went around Cape Horn at the southern tip of South America. The delivery could take as long as six months to arrive in California.

The Gold Rush Draws People West

In 1848, gold was discovered in California. By the mid-1850s, more than 300,000 people had moved to California to search for gold. Some people wanted to keep in contact with friends and family back east.

Others had business to conduct. Six months was too long to wait for mail service.

The US government worked on finding ways to make the mail travel faster. In 1849, they announced plans for the Pacific Mail Steamship Company to deliver mail. Ships brought mail south from the United States over the Atlantic Ocean to the Isthmus of Panama. This area is in the narrow strip of land where North America meets South America. Wagons, mules, and stagecoaches took the mail across land to the other side of the Isthmus. There it was loaded onto a Pacific Mail Steamship

California's Population Explosion

California's gold rush began in 1848. At that time, the non-native population in California was only about 1,000 people. But with the prospect of gold, thousands of people from the East began moving west to find riches. By the end of 1849, there were more than 100,000 non-native people in the area. This huge rise in population led to an increased demand for faster mail service.

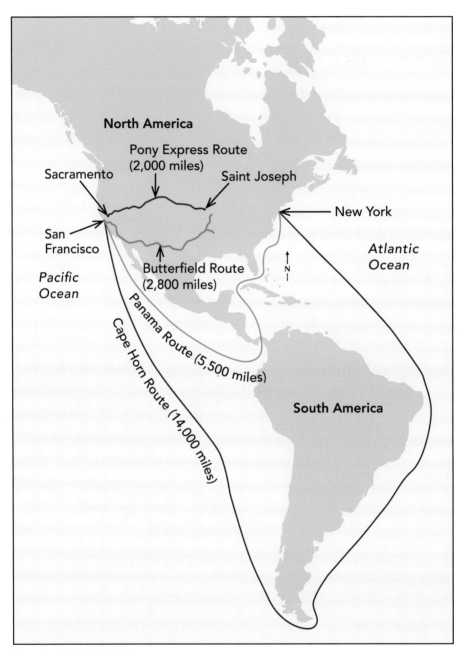

Early US Mail Routes

Find the routes on this map that the mail would take going from east to west before the Pony Express. What caused these routes to be inefficient and take so long?

Company ship. The ship traveled north again through the Pacific Ocean to the United States. This route took at least three weeks. But sometimes it took much longer.

People were still not happy. They wanted mail delivery to take much less than a month. Some tried to carry the mail across the United States itself instead of by sea. Wagon teams were sent West. They followed a northern route used by many gold seekers. But they often broke down or were stopped by bad weather. Sometimes Native Americans who were unhappy that the route passed through their lands also attacked them.

A Southern Mail Route

In 1856, 75,000 Californians sent a petition to Washington, DC. They demanded that the government set up stagecoach mail service to deliver mail more quickly. In 1857, the Post Office awarded a contract to a man named John Butterfield. Butterfield owned a New York stagecoach service. He chose to

Butterfield tried unsuccessfully to make an efficient overland mail route.

take a route across the southern United States. That route avoided some of the northern climates that had slowed earlier mail services. Still, it was nearly 800 miles (1,300 km) longer than the northern route. It also went through Native Americans' lands. They, like tribes in the north, were unhappy about the route passing through.

No matter how hard he tried, John Butterfield could not deliver the mail to the West in less than 23 days. In 1858, silver and more gold were discovered in Colorado and Nevada. More people from the East moved to the West. More people wanted to get mail quickly. Then William Russell from Kansas came up with an idea: a pony relay service.

FURTHER EVIDENCE

Chapter One covers various ideas about why the Pony Express was needed. What is one of the main points of this chapter? What key evidence supports this point? Read the article at the website below. Find a quote on this website that supports the main point you identified. Does the quote support an existing piece of evidence in this chapter? Or does it offer a new piece of evidence?

The Pony Express: Early Mail Delivery
mycorelibrary.com/pony-express

A PONY RELAY SERVICE

William Russell owned a freight and stagecoach company. He found a solution. He would use a relay. Riders would ride horses as quickly as they could. But a horse galloping at full speed could not go very far. So Russell planned for a series of home stations along the route. These stations would provide stopping places for the riders and their horses. Riders would take a new horse and

Fresh horses awaited riders at stations along the route.

gallop to the next station. After a rider had traveled 75–100 miles (120–160 km), a new rider with a fresh horse would meet him at a station. The new rider would take the mailbag and ride off. The first rider and his horse would rest. They waited for a return rider to come. But there were many challenges to this plan.

Stations

There were 157 stations along the Pony Express route. Generally there was a station every 5–20 miles (8–32 km). There were two kinds of stations. Swing stations were places for a rider to switch to a fresh horse. Home stations were farther apart. They had beds for the riders to rest. These stations usually had an agent who stayed there to help the riders. There were fewer home stations than swing stations. Riders were expected to change horses more often than they could rest themselves.

Unfamiliar Lands

The Pony Express riders rode alone. That was dangerous for many reasons. Most knew little about the land in the West. There was little help along the way. Pioneers had traveled to

Riders rode beyond the telegraph lines into land populated by few other Americans.

the West Coast. But very few had settled in any area in between. Kansas, Nebraska, Colorado, Wyoming, Utah, and Nevada were not states yet. That meant there were few towns or established roads. Other than the home stations, there were not many places to stop. They slept on the ground outdoors if they were tired. They survived on only the food and water they carried. Few settlements also meant little variety in food. There were no stores. Food had to be hauled from long distances. Often all riders had to eat were beans, bacon, corn bread, and coffee.

The terrain between Missouri and California varied greatly. Riders would travel through deserts, forests, and mountains with no trails and lots of snow and ice. They saw many kinds of wildlife. Some, such as wolves, could be dangerous. And they only had themselves to rely on.

Threatening Weather

The weather was another challenge. Deserts could be unbearably hot, with little water available. Sandstorms

The Pony Express ran through many landscapes, including deserts.

and snowstorms made it very hard to see. That could be very dangerous in the mountains.

Conditions could be harsh. William Campbell was a rider who told his life story to a New York University professor. For a full day and night, he rode 120 miles (190 km) toward Fairfield, Utah. The snow was up to three feet (1 m) deep, and the air was cold. He had to lead his horse because the trail was so hard to see.

Tensions with Native Americans

Tension between the mail service and Native Americans also put riders at risk. Few people working with the Pony Express knew the Native Americans who lived between Missouri and California. Some Native Americans were upset that the route ran through their land. Station workers did not always try to be peaceful with them. And

PERSPECTIVES
Advertising for Riders

The people who put the Pony Express together understood the risks and problems of the route. It has been said that an ad seeking riders was placed in a newspaper. The ad said: "Wanted—young, skinny, wiry fellows, not over eighteen. Must be expert riders, willing to risk death daily. Orphans preferred." It is not certain if this ad was really published. But the story highlights how difficult the ride was known to be.

Pony Express stations were easy targets. They were often located in isolated areas. There were also many conflicts between US Army troops and Native Americans. Some Native Americans were angry at how white people destroyed trees that Native Americans gathered nuts from. They attacked white people and Pony Express stations. The US Army fought back. The conflicts threatened to disrupt the Pony Express.

EXPLORE ONLINE

Chapter Two talks about the creation of the Pony Express. The article at the website below goes into more detail about this. How does the information on the website compare to the information in Chapter Two? What new information did you learn from the website?

Making the Pony Express

mycorelibrary.com/pony-express

CHAPTER THREE

THE PONY EXPRESS MAKES ITS DEBUT

Serving as a Pony Express rider was a dangerous job. But Johnny Fry was willing to try it. He rode through the streets of Saint Joseph as people cheered him on. When he got to the edge of town, he arrived at the banks of the Missouri River. He and his horse boarded a ferry that took them across the river to Kansas. From there, Fry rode 90 miles (145 km) as quickly as he could. He stopped at swing stations to

Fry left Saint Joseph and raced for the Missouri River.

Waiting without Word

During the 11 days of the first Pony Express ride from Saint Joseph to Sacramento, there was no way for the riders to let people know how they were doing. No one in either Saint Joseph or Sacramento knew if the riders were keeping the planned schedule. No one knew if a rider had been hurt along the way. Even the riders who were waiting at home stations did not know when—or even if— the rider who was supposed to meet them would actually arrive. It was not until the westbound rider reached the Sierra Nevada, where there were telegraph lines, that word could be sent.

get fresh horses. At the end of his 90 miles, he stopped at a home station to rest. Another rider picked up the mochila and rode out.

Other Pony Express riders duplicated the speedy ride 307 times. They rode through many landscapes, always alone.

The Great American Desert

In Kansas, a rider entered what was called the Great American Desert. Today that area is known as the Great Plains. This part of the United States is very flat. It made for fast

The Great Plains are an expanse of grassland.

riding. A rider went through Nebraska to Julesburg, Colorado, sometimes traveling along the North Platte River. Then he would turn north to reach Fort Laramie, Wyoming.

The Rocky Mountains

Once the mail reached Fort Laramie, it was at the end of the Great American Desert. This meant that the flat, easy part of the trip was over. Ahead of the rider were the Rocky Mountains. He crossed the mountains using the South Pass, where the ascent is gentle.

The Great Salt Lake Desert

Once the rider descended from the Rockies, it was not long before he reached Salt Lake City. West from Salt Lake City was an actual desert: the Great Salt Lake Desert. Unlike the so-called Great American Desert, which was flat land but could sustain farm crops, the Great Salt Lake Desert was dry. It could get hot in the summer. But in April, it could still be cold. Winds whipped the sand around, making visibility difficult. If it was cold enough, there would be snow.

The Fierce Sierra Nevada

The desert eventually gave way to northern Nevada. The terrain here was not as difficult, but it led to the

Sierra Nevada. Crossing those mountains would bring the rider to Sacramento, California. The Sierra Nevada were rugged. They could have significant amounts of snow on them almost half of the year. Many Pony Express riders felt that crossing the Sierra Nevada was the worst part of the trip—worse than facing attacks from Native Americans, crossing the desert in the summer heat, or trying to cross rivers swollen from spring rains.

Excellent Service

In spite of all the potential problems along the way, the first Pony Express riders were anxious to meet their goal. On April 13, 1860, the final rider, William Hamilton, arrived in Sacramento. It was close to midnight. Large

The Cost of Mailing a Letter

The Pony Express was very fast, but it was also very expensive. When the Pony Express began, the cost to mail a .5-ounce (14 g) letter to California was five dollars. In today's dollars, this would be over $100. In 2016 it cost 47 cents to mail a 1-ounce (28-g) letter anywhere in the United States.

Riders considered the Sierra Nevada the most dangerous part of the trip.

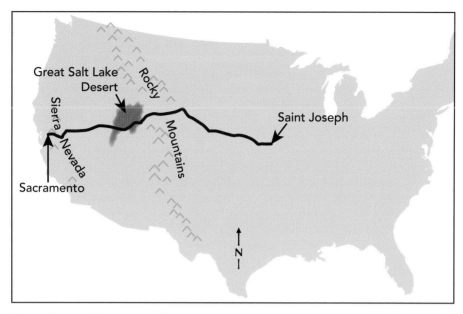

The Pony Express Route

Pony Express riders had to travel a very long way through all kinds of terrain. This map shows just how far they had to go. It also shows the mountains they had to cross. Which areas do you think were easier to travel? Which were harder?

crowds of people waved flags and cheered. Church towers rang bells. The local fire department fired a cannon in celebration. The Pony Express had done what no other mail service had been able to do. It had delivered the mail across almost 2,000 miles (3,200 km) in only 11 days. Hamilton told the newspaper that he thought the riders could make

Californians greeted Pony Express rider Hamilton with a celebration.

even better time in the summer. Some of the trails in April were very muddy, which had slowed them down.

The future looked bright for the Pony Express. People in both the East and the West were excited to have quick mail service. But the Pony Express would only last a year and a half.

The conditions that riders faced were difficult. Without good roads and trails, the ride could be hard and even dangerous. Adolph Sutro writes about an encounter with a Pony Express Rider:

> The storm grew fiercer and fiercer as we went on: the flakes of snow and hail were blowing into our faces with such power that they stung like needles, and nearly blinded us. The lofty pine trees swung to and fro, and the noise of the wind breaking through their branches, creaking and howling, was truly fearful. Our poor animals instinctively knew that they had to hurry on, and on we went, as if fleeing before a terrible enemy. . . . On the very summit, we met a lonely rider dashing along at a tremendous rate. We wondered what could possibly induce him to go on through that gale, and thought it must be some important business. It was the Pony Express.

> Source: "Pony Express News (1860–61)." XP Pony Express Home Station. The National Pony Express Association, n.d. Web. Accessed April 20, 2016.

Back It Up

The author of this passage is using evidence to make a point. Write a paragraph describing the point the author is making. Then write down two or three pieces of evidence the author uses to make the point.

CHAPTER FOUR

A RAPID RISE AND FALL

The Pony Express seemed like a wonderful solution to a big problem. But the solution itself created some new problems. It also had competition.

The Pony Express had only been in business a little over a month when conflict slowed its deliveries. Three brothers from Maine lived at Williams Station in Nevada. Williams Station was a stagecoach station and general store. It was not a Pony Express stop.

The Paiutes had endured a harsh winter from 1859–1860. A shrinking food supply caused by white settlers was partially to blame.

James Williams had been away from the station. But on May 8, 1860, he returned to find his brothers dead. There were other bodies, too. The station had been burned to the ground, and all the animals they had were gone.

This was the beginning of the Paiute Indian War. It is sometimes called the Pyramid Lake Uprising because it was close to Pyramid Lake. James Williams immediately left to warn other stations that he believed the Paiutes were responsible for the deaths.

But journalist Dan De Quille, who lived in the area at the time, uncovered the truth. Men at the Williams Station had kidnapped two Paiute girls. A Paiute man came to rescue the women. He was not able to do so by himself. He returned to his tribe for help. These men burned down the station and killed the station workers. The Paiutes were angry. Paiute women had been abused. White people had also been felling trees that provided the Paiute with winter food. The Pony Express was partly to blame.

The kidnapping sparked a war between the Paiutes and white settlers. The war sometimes delayed the Pony Express.

The Paiutes targeted and destroyed Pony Express stations in May and early June. During May, Pony Express rider Bob Haslam rode 380 miles (611 km) back and forth between stations when another rider refused to. The other rider was afraid of the Paiutes. There were days when some of the routes could not run. Finally the military was sent in to escort riders. The US Army began to fight the Paiutes. Americans quickly found out they had underestimated the tribe. A cease-fire was reached in August 1860.

But traveling alone by horseback through wilderness and all kinds of weather was a danger that never disappeared.

Losing Money

Finances were another trouble. Even though the Pony Express charged a high price for its services, it had many expenses. It cost a great deal of money to build stations, acquire horses, supply the riders, and pay the men. They also had to rebuild

Completion of the transcontinental telegraph lines ended the Pony Express's service.

stations destroyed in the war. The company needed about $1,000 per day to run the service. However, its high prices kept many people from using the Pony Express. They did not have enough business to cover their costs. The Pony Express lost money almost from the beginning.

New Technology

The final blow to the Pony Express came from improved technology. While the riders raced back and forth across the western half of the United States, other workers moved west as well. Telegraph lines that reached from the East Coast to Missouri were being extended. By October 24, 1861, transcontinental telegraph lines were completed. People could now send messages much more quickly than by Pony Express. It was also safer. Mail was more likely to get lost when sent by horseback through dangerous conditions.

During its brief run, the Pony Express delivered about 35,000 letters.

The End of the Pony Express

Two days after the transcontinental telegraph was completed, the Pony Express announced that it was going to shut down the service. There were still a few riders on the trail, delivering their last pieces of mail. During its 18 months, the Pony Express had filled a major gap in mail delivery. But that gap had not lasted long. Even if the telegraph had not taken over, it is unlikely the Pony Express could have continued since it was losing so much money.

But for a short time, Americans thought of the Pony Express riders as heroes. The riders braved all kinds of dangers to bring the mail to people more quickly than ever before. They risked their lives to help the East keep in contact with the West.

By the Numbers

In only 18 months, the Pony Express

- made 308 complete runs
- delivered 34,753 letters
- lost only one mochila
- traveled a total of about 616,000 miles (991,000 km), which amounts to circling Earth 30 times
- employed 80 men and 500 horses
- built 200 stations

Paiutes and other bands of Native Americans met in May 1860. Many Native Americans wanted to go to war with white people. White people, including those connected with the Pony Express, were causing resources the Native Americans relied on to disappear. But Numaga of the Pyramid tribe thought war with white people would lead to their destruction:

> They will come like the sand in a whirlwind and drive you from your homes. You will be forced among the barren rocks of the north, where your ponies will die; where you will see the women and old men starve, and listen to the cries of your children for food.

> Source: Ferol Egan. Sand in a Whirlwind: The Paiute Indian War of 1860. Reno, NV: University of Nevada Press, 2003. Print. 102.

Changing Minds

This passage discusses reasons one Native American did not want to go to war. Take a position on going to war, then imagine that your best friend has the opposite opinion. Write a short essay trying to change your friend's mind. Make sure you detail your opinion and your reasons for it. Include facts and details that support your reasons.

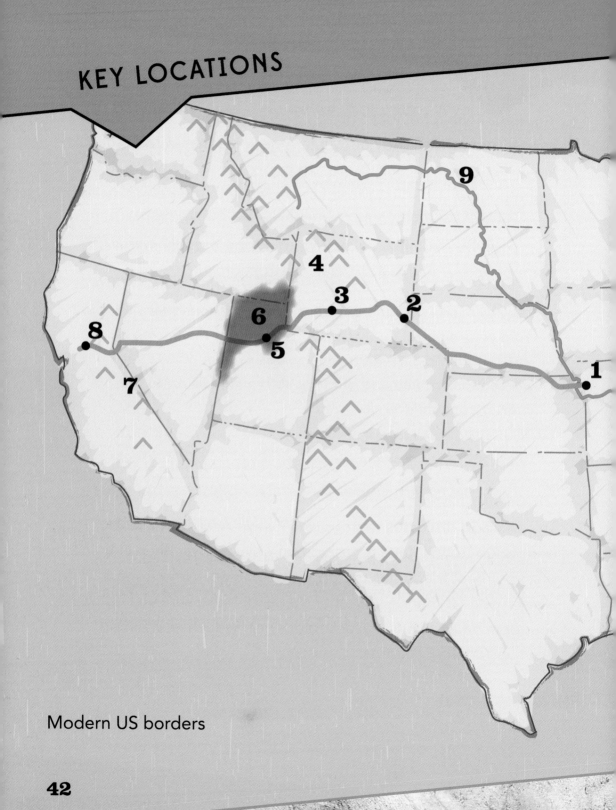

Modern US borders

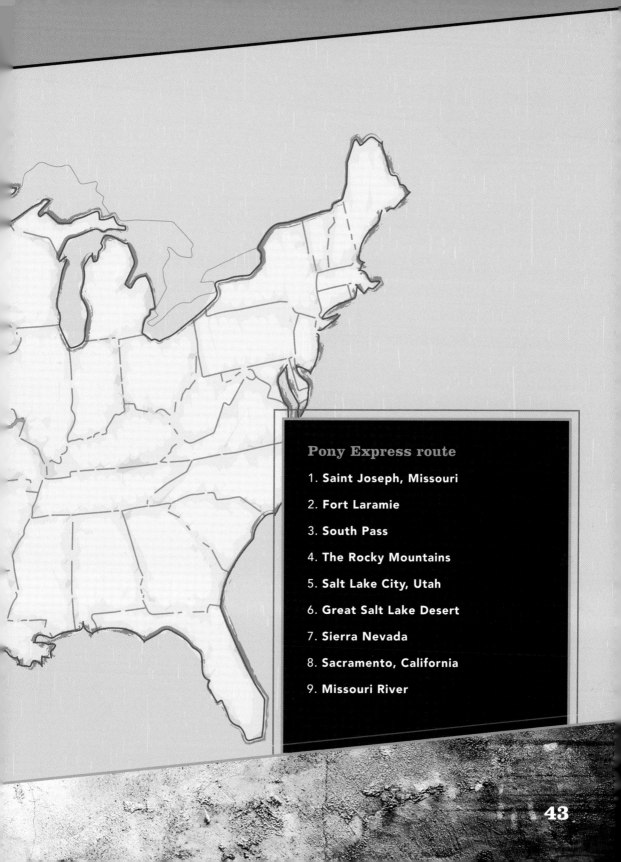

Pony Express route

1. **Saint Joseph, Missouri**

2. **Fort Laramie**

3. **South Pass**

4. **The Rocky Mountains**

5. **Salt Lake City, Utah**

6. **Great Salt Lake Desert**

7. **Sierra Nevada**

8. **Sacramento, California**

9. **Missouri River**

STOP AND THINK

Say What?

Studying the Pony Express can mean learning a lot of new vocabulary. Find five words in this book you have never heard before. Use a dictionary to find out what they mean. Then write the meanings in your own words, and use each word in a new sentence.

Surprise Me

Chapter One talks about the difficulties of getting mail across the United States in the 1800s. It also talks about the different ways mail was delivered. After reading this chapter, what two or three ideas did you find most surprising? Write a few sentences about each idea. Why did you find each one surprising?

Tell the Tale

Chapter Three discusses the route the first riders took. Imagine you are one of the first Pony Express riders. Write 200 words about the journey. What do you see? How do you feel?

Dig Deeper

After reading this book, what questions do you still have about the Pony Express? With an adult's help, find a few reliable sources that can help answer your questions. Write a paragraph about what you learned.

GLOSSARY

gunfighter
an outlaw or lawman who was highly skilled with a gun and used it to solve arguments

isthmus
a narrow strip of land that connects two larger pieces of land

journalist
someone who writes articles for the media, such as a newspaper or magazine

prospect
something expected or looked forward to in the future

sandstorm
a storm in a desert where strong winds blow sand around and make it hard to see

stagecoach
a large carriage pulled by horses that carried passengers and mail along established routes

telegraph
the use of wires and electrical signals to send messages over long distances

terrain
the physical features of a piece of land

transcontinental
going across a continent

tribes
groups of people who have the same language, customs, beliefs, and often the same ancestors

LEARN MORE

Books

Gray-Kanatiiosh, Barbara A. *Paiute*. Edina, MN: Abdo Publishing, 2007.

Holub, Joan. *What Was the Gold Rush?* New York: Grosset & Dunlap, 2013.

Thompson, Gare. *Riding with the Mail: The Story of the Pony Express.* Washington, DC: National Geographic Society, 2007.

Websites

To learn more about the Wild West, visit **booklinks.abdopublishing.com**. These links are routinely monitored and updated to provide the most current information available.

Visit **mycorelibrary.com** for free additional tools for teachers and students.

INDEX

ABOUT THE AUTHOR

Amy C. Rea grew up in northern Minnesota and now lives in a Minneapolis suburb with her husband, two sons, and dog. She's written about the lost colonists of Roanoke and the lost continent of Atlantis.